Contents

Introduction

People largely seek happiness through the pursuit of pleasure and the avoidance of pain. This approach is hardwired into our species and there's nothing wrong with it except that it is unreliable—it doesn't really work. What really makes us happy is when we follow what our spirit wants to do, regardless of whether it causes us pleasure or pain. If you follow what your spirit wants, you will always be happy whether things are going your way or not! A lot of folks these days don't have a clear idea of how to get in touch with their spirit, so what follows are seven core practices that will get you in touch with your spirit and make you truly happy, followed by several tips that simply make day-to-day life easier and more fun.

7 core practices that will make you a happier person

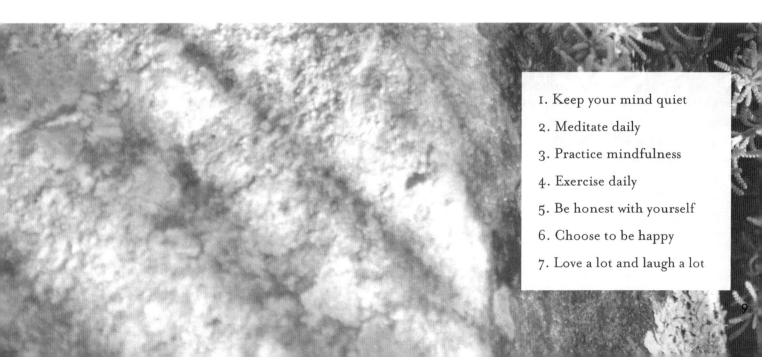

1. Keep your mind quiet
2. Meditate daily
3. Practice mindfulness
4. Exercise daily
5. Be honest with yourself
6. Choose to be happy
7. Love a lot and laugh a lot

1. Keep your mind quiet

If there's only one thing in this book you pay attention to, this should be it. Our incessant internal dialogue—all of the strategizing, defending, regurgitating and worrying that we do—covers our true nature. When you stop thought, you directly experience that you are made of light, Consciousness, God (you choose your favorite word).

Keeping the mind quiet won't make you unconscious or an idiot. Rather you become wiser as you begin to see the vast wisdom that is at your core. You'll find that you begin to understand things without having to think them through and that you have access to greater knowledge that isn't available to you when your mind is a cyclone of thoughts and concerns.

But keeping your mind quiet is hard to do in our digital, socially-networked world, where we are constantly bombarded with information and never out of reach from…anyone! How do you do it? The answer is simple—you meditate.

2. Meditate daily

Meditation calms you down. It chills you out. It makes you sharper and smarter. It can improve your health and make you feel younger. But most importantly, *it makes you happy!*

When you meditate you go into the light inside of you, the light that makes up everything and everyone. It's the light of eternity and it's happiness itself. So when you meditate, you are making yourself more available to the light in your being, which literally makes you happy!

When you meditate you come to have silent knowledge about the universe that makes some of the seemingly harsh and random events of life more understandable. You come to see that you are not just your body and your mind, but that there is a part of you that lives beyond the death of the body. You see that who you truly are is eternal.

This might sound simplistic or fantastical, so you have to check it out for yourself to see that it is true. In fact, one of the reasons I like the practice of meditation is that it's not about blindly believing what someone preaches to you, but rather finding out for yourself what is true.

For meditation instruction, refer to *How to Meditate* in the appendix.

3. Practice mindfulness

Mindfulness is the process of watching what is passing through your mind and stopping the thoughts that are draining or unhealthy. Most things only need to be thought through once. The rest of the thinking, the mulling over and obsessing, is not only draining, it actually makes it harder to objectively see what is best. When you keep your mind quiet and don't play your worries, schemes and dreams over and over again, you create space for inner knowledge to bubble up and be heard.

Mindfulness isn't limited to stopping negative or repetitive thoughts, it also includes not holding conversations in your mind with people you know. A lot of people talk to other people in their minds, explaining their beliefs and defending their positions. Not only is this a waste of energy, again it prevents your mind from being still. When your mind is still you can more clearly see the pointers in the universe. The universe gives us all kinds of information, but you have to be still to see it. When your mind is going round and round defending your ego, you miss these pointers, not to mention the relaxation and brightness that comes from being still.

The good news is that after practicing mindfulness for a while it becomes automatic, so as negative or repetitive thoughts and inner conversations arise, you naturally stop them and redirect your mind to higher, calmer thoughts or no thoughts at all.

4. Exercise daily

Everyone knows that exercise helps the physical body, but it also really helps clear out our non-physical energy body. In the course of our daily lives we pick up all kinds of stuff—stress from commuting, tiredness from dealing with family, friends or coworkers who are having a hard time, stress from relationship, work or financial woes or simply having too much to do. Exercise helps blow out this buildup, so it makes us feel much happier. If you think of your aura as acting like a sponge that absorbs the feelings and thoughts of those you interact with, exercise is like rinsing and squeezing out that sponge. Women in particular benefit from daily exercise because they pick up even more auric garbage than men.

The type of exercise regimen you follow depends on your level of fitness and your demeanor. What's important is to find a type of exercise that you enjoy so it's not something you dread doing. It helps to alternate what exercise you do so you don't get bored, and for those who are on stationary equipment like an elliptic trainer or treadmill, it's great to watch DVDs or digital downloads. If you haven't exercised in a while, it's a good idea to consult your doctor before you start up again. She can advise you on a good regimen for your age and fitness level.

5. Be honest with yourself

Honesty with yourself is essential to being happy. You have to check that what you are doing in your life is working for you. Sometimes we have such a strong idea of how our life should be and what will make us happy that we don't want to face that these ideas aren't right for us anymore. We may have grown out of them or they may have never been our ideas and dreams in the first place, but instead were imposed by family or society and accepted by us as ours. Other times we have invested so much time and energy to get our life to where it is, that we don't want to face the fact that it is no longer working. When we honestly recognize that something is no longer working, then from this place of recognition we can begin to change it.

Being honest about what is working applies to all aspects of your life, big and small—whether it's recognizing that you're bored with your job and you need to mix it up, or that constantly checking your phone diffuses your focus and you need to dial it down. When you recognize what is not working in your life and change it, despite past ideas of what you think will make you happy, you will be a happier person.

Note that you don't have to necessarily share or discuss your internal honesty with others. In fact, if we had to share all our internal insights with others, we'd never be completely honest with ourselves! What matters is that you are simply honest with yourself.

20

6. Choose to be happy

It's a personal choice to be happy. Everyone has a high, happy side and a low, bored or depressed side, and which side you live in is determined by the choices you make. The choices that lead to happiness are the ones that challenge us, awaken us, and keep us balanced. They are the choices to meditate and work-out when you'd rather watch TV, to be mindful when you'd rather obsess on something negative, to work on your career when it seems easier to just hang out where you are, and also the choice to relax and unwind when you know you need that but are nonetheless tempted to stay plugged in. The choices that lead to happiness are the ones that take care of the things that are yours to take care of and, just as importantly, the choices to not take on things that are not your responsibility. On a daily basis, we are presented with numerous choices, both simple and complex, that lead us to either more happiness or less. When you become the person who makes the higher choice by default, you will absolutely feel happier. The good news is that meditation increases your powers of discrimination and will, so it's easier to both discern the higher choice and follow it.

Of course, many of the physical circumstances of our lives are beyond our control, but even in these situations there is a choice to be happy. When you get caught in a major traffic delay, you can bemoan your fate which magnifies the misery of the situation, or you can keep on hand great audio books, podcasts and music to entertain yourself while you are trapped in your car. In more dire situations, like finding out your partner cheated on you or that you have been diagnosed with cancer, there is still an opportunity to be happy. Stick with me for a moment on this one. Sometimes the most painful situations in life can act as a catalyst to finally get us to really stop thought, go into our inner light and experience that we are not who we think we are—to see that we're made of light and are eternal. This is the happiest of all experiences. When everything is going our way we tend to not be very introspective, but in truly unpleasant times, in our disillusionment with how we thought our life would go, there is an opening to experience something deeper. So even amidst the crappiest situation, there is a choice to indulge in the difficulties of your life or an option to go deeper into the quiet and deeper into your soul where true happiness resides. True happiness isn't about everything working out your way. It's really about being in touch with your inner light.

scotties

les artistes

7. Love a lot and laugh a lot

When we love, light comes through our being and brightens us, lightens us and makes us feel happy. The love you express doesn't have to be towards another person, it can be towards a great number of things—pets, plants, your artwork, sports, challenging experiences. In fact, love has very little to do with a person. It comes from us and it grows the more we love. We are happy when we love. We are unhappy when we stop loving.

Similarly, when we laugh, we relax and light flows through us more easily. It brightens us and makes us feel happy. Laughter and lightheartedness are great balms for our body, mind and soul. When we laugh a lot we are happier people. (It should be pointed out however that laughing at others, their misfortunes, sorrow or pain, will in no way make you happy. This lack of compassion actually decreases the amount of light flowing through you.)

Tips that make everyday life easier and more fun

Live in an area with good energy.

Where you choose to live is extremely important. There are some places on the planet that have better energy than others. Places with good energy make you feel better, more awake and more inspired. Everything seems brighter, edges seem more defined. Places with less energy make you feel dull, sleepy, even hopeless. This may sound strange at first but when you think back on specific places you have visited and how you have felt uplifted or dulled by them, you can see how where you live affects your day-to-day energy level and happiness. With this in mind, it makes sense to spend more money for a place with good energy than to spend less for a physically similar place that doesn't have much energy. The savings from living in an energetically low neighborhood cost you in many other ways, but primarily in that you don't have the energy or inspiration to do whatever it is you want to do! That being said, be sure not to spend more than you can afford on your living space, since living above your means is one of the shortest paths to stress, worry and unhappiness.

To find a house or apartment that works for you, pay attention to how you feel when you are in the place. If a place has a lot of positives and fits your needs from a practical perspective, but something just doesn't click despite it seeming right in every way, it's not the right place. On the other hand, if you walk in and feel a smile on your face and think "Yes!," this is a good place for you. This methodology may sound childish, but it is your non-physical body that is assessing the energy of the place. This part of you is more intelligent than your mind and is better at assessing energy. After you try this method and see how well it works, you will lose your skepticism.

De-clutter your house.

Keep your house clean and clutter-free. The state of your house (or any environment such as your office or car) is a reflection of your mind, so it's easier to keep your mind quiet when your house is in order. When you clean out old and unused items from your house, you will feel much lighter and find there is more energy and excitement to do the things you want to do, and more space for new ideas to bubble up.

When you de-clutter your house, be sure to get rid of unwanted items people have given you. You shouldn't keep a gift you don't like out of obligation because you feel that obligation or distaste when you look at it.

Remove emotionally heavy items from your house.

Objects can have people and memories associated with them, and if these associations are sad, depressing, angry or make you feel bad for any reason, then get rid of those things. When you have items in your house that have heavy associations with them, a part of your mind feels the heaviness every time you look at them and it drags you down. Getting rid of these items is one of the quickest and easiest ways to feel better on a day-to-day basis.

Some examples of emotionally heavy items to get rid of, such as jewelry or gifts from old lovers or the bed you shared with an ex, are pretty intuitive and most people get rid of these naturally. Less obvious are items that have associations with people you love, but don't make you feel good. For example, one woman I know always felt uncomfortable in her living room, so avoided it. She described the room as having fairly standard living room furniture and about twenty to thirty family photos on the mantel and piano. After some questioning, I realized the photos made her nostalgic and sad about the passage of time. Though she is quite close with her children who are now adults, and doesn't want to go back to the times captured in the pictures even if she could, the photos made her sad. I suggested she box up the photos and put them in a closet as an experiment to see if it would make the room feel better. She put the photos away and was amazed at how much lighter and more enjoyable the room felt. You know there is no rule that says you have to have pictures of your kids or relatives or any other thing in your house. If something makes you feel weird, for whatever reason, then get rid of it. There are social conventions about what the house of a good friend, mom, partner, etc. looks like, but these are just imposed ideas that you don't have to follow. If something makes you feel heavy, get rid of it!

If you feel too attached to an item that you think you should get rid of, put it in a box in an out of the way place and see what it's like to live without it. Most people find they don't miss the object at all and end up getting rid of it.

When you move into a house, push the previous occupants' energy out.

When people live in a house their mind states and patterns get embedded in the house. Since you don't want to take on other people's thoughts and patterns (especially if they're negative, angry, alcoholic, overly hungry, etc.), you need to push the previous occupants' energy out. To do this, clean the house thoroughly, paint the walls, and either replace or steam clean the carpets. This initial investment of time when you first move in really pays off. You'll feel better the entire time you live there.

Follow the 7-second rule.

You have about 7 – 10 seconds before a thought gets stuck in your mind. When a negative or unhealthy thought arises, redirect your mind immediately before the thought gets stuck in a tape loop in your mind.

If you're having a difficult time redirecting your thoughts, you can immerse your mind in a magazine, newspaper or book; you can listen to audio books or talk radio, or work on a project or hobby that completely absorbs you—whatever it takes to substitute the negative or stressful thought with something higher. (Music alone is usually not effective as an aide in mindfulness because your mind can still easily wander while listening to music.) For those who have a spiritual teacher they love, the most powerful and effective way to still the mind is to move your mind to an image of him or her.

Using this technique of switching your mind away from a negative or stressful thought before it takes hold isn't meant to imply that you shouldn't address the issue that is causing the troublesome thought. Instead the technique is useful when there is no action that can be taken at the time and the best thing to do is push the thought out of your mind. For example, if you are unemployed and looking for a job, you should of course do everything you can to find a job. However, once you've done all you can for the day, it doesn't help your search to worry about it at night since worrying drains your energy. So as worry starts to seep in, employ the 7-second rule to keep it at bay. Another example is, suppose you and your partner broke up after many years together and when you think of him or her, it makes you feel really sad. In this case, employ this technique when you notice the thought of your ex creeping into your mind, so you can prevent the thought of him or her from getting stuck in your mind.

Follow the energy.

When you are making changes or moves in your life, follow the option where you feel more energy. Sometimes one choice will feel flat, while another choice that may not make as much practical sense has a flood of positive energy behind it. When you follow the one with energy, you are following the option that is more correct for you and it will lead to something better than you could have imagined.

Please note that you have to be honest with yourself on this tip. It is not meant to be taken impractically. For instance, unless you're independently wealthy, you shouldn't weigh options like whether there is more energy in accepting a job you're not excited about versus not working. In this instance, if there isn't a job that has energy, you should take the one you're not excited about. You will be much happier being able to pay the bills than being unemployed and broke. Then in the meantime, you can search for a career that has more energy and is more exciting to you.

Use jealousy to show you what you should be working on.

Jealousy has nothing to do with the person you are jealous of. When you feel jealous of someone, the feeling is really pointing to the fact that it's time for you to work for the thing you're jealous of. For instance, if a friend tells you about a jump she made in her career and you feel a twinge of jealousy, it means you need to make a jump in your career or in your life. It doesn't mean that you need to make the same kind of jump, but rather that you need to look at whether you're being too complacent in your life and whether it is time to step it up by taking new classes, getting a new certification, writing a book, etc.

Now don't confuse jealousy with the feeling you have when people try to make you envious of them by broadcasting how fabulous their lives are. Anyone who is trying to win the envy of others is usually quite insecure and is doing it to squash a feeling of inadequacy they have. People who are rich, beautiful or smart that are confident, don't try to make you envious of them. The best response to someone who is trying to do this is to not react at all, but if you need to react than you can feel compassion for their insecurity.

Don't knock others who are successful. The only person you should be competitive with is yourself.

There is enough success for everyone, so there is no need to knock someone else's success. You can use other people's accomplishments to inspire you, but being competitive with others isn't helpful because it shifts your state of mind to a more primitive one based on fear and territoriality, which isn't a happy place to live inside your mind. Besides, being competitive with others doesn't help you win anyway. In fact, you'll be more "in the zone" and perform better when you just focus on your own work without the distraction of monitoring your competition.

Continually challenge and refine yourself.

We are happier when we are challenged. There's so much energy in continually refining and challenging ourselves in our career, sports, hobbies, relationships—really all aspects of our lives. Being bored is one of the most draining states of mind there is. When we think back on the most interesting and exciting times in our lives, we recall times when we were pushing ourselves to a new level—when we were working furiously to get a new pitch complete for a competition, when we were working on a term paper and new connections were formed we hadn't seen before, when we organized a complicated event or when we learned to play an instrument. Even though part of us thinks we'll be happy lazing around, if we're honest, we get empowered by learning new concepts and new skills. When we're not stretching ourselves, we get bored and feel drained in fairly short order.

Become financially independent.

People make incredibly bad decisions that lead to a lot of unhappiness when they aren't financially independent. They'll marry someone they don't love or stay with a partner or spouse they don't like solely because they don't have the financial wherewithal to do what they really want to do. When you are financially independent and are not beholden to a parent, partner or spouse's agenda or idea for your life, you are free to follow the choices that are appropriate for you, which is an amazingly freeing and happy feeling!

The foundation of financial independence is a good career, combined with the ability to budget and manage your money. You need to be able to support yourself in the style that keeps you from making a bad decision you wouldn't make if money wasn't an issue. So while some careers may be easier or more accessible, they may not provide the kind of income you need long-term and therefore won't allow you to be as independent as when you choose a more lucrative career. However, having a solid income is not enough, you also need the ability to save and grow the money you make. If you don't save any of your money, then you undermine your independence and quality of life in your retirement years. I'm not pretending that if you aren't already financially independent that you won't have to make radical changes in your life, such as going back to school, starting your own company, living on a smaller budget or stop letting your partner or spouse handle all the finances, but the payoff of not being dependent on anyone else financially is huge!

If you miss the first bus, catch the next one.

If you miss an opportunity or mess one up, don't give up, just catch the next "bus." There will always be other opportunities, no matter how we've messed up in the past. We don't just get one shot—life isn't that chintzy. Other opportunities will be available, though they will most likely take a different form than the previous one.

Analyze mistakes to learn how to avoid making them again, and then move on.

Don't wallow in a mistake you made in the past by feeling bad or guilty. These sentiments won't help you make changes or improvements and can actually drain or even immobilize you. Instead, analyze the mistake, identify what didn't work and what you need to do differently going forward, then move on.

Expect some people to be unhappy about positive changes you are making.

When you are making positive changes in your life, some people, be they partners, parents, siblings, friends or coworkers, won't like the change and will try to shoot it down. Sometimes it's because your changes make them feel bad that they aren't moving forward themselves. Other times it's because the changes don't fit into their idea of your relationship and they're afraid they are going to lose you. Whatever the reason, if you are aware of the dynamic, it's easier to deal with.

Avoid naysayers.

There are some people who have limited perception and don't think it's possible to change your circumstances or make your dreams come true. Avoid sharing your dreams and aspirations with these folks because they can drag you down with their negativity and dissuade you from working towards your goals. Instead seek constructive criticism and feedback from people who are happy to assist you and don't want to shoot you down.

> "
> To know what you prefer instead of humbly saying 'Amen' to what the world tells you you ought to prefer, is to have kept your soul alive."
>
> Robert Louis Stevenson

Don't let the fear of offending someone trap you in a draining situation.

If someone is dumping all over you, you don't need to stick around because you feel like you will hurt that person's feelings by leaving quickly. This may seem incredibly obvious, yet many people will allow a coworker to dump all their garbage on them, or allow a creepy man to hit on them because they don't want to hurt his feelings. It's okay to hurt the feelings of someone who is draining you or dumping on you! If you want to be graceful in your escape, you can have a few good excuses in your back pocket, such as "I was just on my way to the restroom" or "I have a meeting that I need to get to," but don't take on someone's bad energy because you think it is the polite or compassionate thing to do.

Don't waste time waiting for someone to save you.

You have probably heard the expression that life is what happens to you while you're waiting for your ship to come in. If you're looking for someone to sweep into your life and save you from your unhappiness, you are simply postponing your happiness. No one else can make you happy. Certainly there are people that are fun to be around, and there are people who have money that makes some things in life more comfortable, but expecting another person to be the source of your happiness keeps you from doing the work that will bring energy and happiness into your life right now. You'll be happier if you quit waiting for that ship to come in and just take control of what you need to do to feel happy. Don't take a back seat role in your own life!

Let relationships go when they are no longer appropriate for you.

People change over time and in different ways, so that someone you were great friends with at one point may not be a good fit anymore. There's so much romanticization around the beauty of lasting friendships that we may feel obligated to spend time with people that we don't really enjoy anymore. Let them go.

Protect your important relationships.

Likewise, take steps to protect the relationships that are most important to you. When you are in a situation where you can say something that you know will hurt the relationship, you simply don't. I'm not referring to true issues that need to be discussed, but rather the myriad of petty things we say to friends and loved ones to prove that we're right, our way is more sensible, we have better taste, etc. These petty comments erode our relationships and aren't worth it when we really care about the relationship.

Lay the groundwork that allows the universe to help you.

You have to create structures that allow the energy of the universe to come through and help you. For instance, if you are looking for a job, you have to work on your resume and make it impeccable, then strategically distribute it and meet with agencies, contacts, etc. You have to lay the ground work which will allow the universe to provide you with the perfect job. No one is going to call you out of the blue and offer you a job if they don't even know you exist! Similarly, if you are looking for a new place to live, the universe will provide the perfect place for your circumstances, but again you have to do the ground work—you have to look at the ads and go visit places. If you ask, the universe will definitely help you out, but you have to do your part to make it manifest.

Be a beginner.

When you have the state of mind of a beginner, you allow yourself to try new things and are open to new ideas, which is energizing and fun. When you are a beginner, you're not afraid to try something just because you won't be good at it or because it's "not you." You can have a great time at something and do it without the intent of becoming an expert. Who doesn't love and admire the eighty-one-year-old woman who is picking up the piano for the first time or the fifty-year-old who is just learning to surf, both of whom are unlikely to become experts in these fields.

When you have the mind state of an expert and are heavy with success, you're more likely to stay in your comfort zone and limit your experiences to those in which you can excel, and obviously that is not a fun way to live. And even in the fields in which you are truly an expert, it's always great to not know it all. In being open we create room to learn new things and refine and improve our knowledge and skills.

Finally, and perhaps most importantly, life is simply harder when you approach it as a know-it-all. When we think back on times when we "knew it all," we invariably created more work for ourselves. I recall a time at one of my first jobs, the sous-chef saw me laboriously chopping an onion and said, "Hey, let me show you a great way to quickly dice an onion." I replied, "I already know how" and summarily cut off the opportunity to learn how to do something in a more efficient way. At some point, I did learn the professional way to dice an onion and was amazed at what an idiot I had been. In "knowing it all," I looked like an idiot to my coworkers by clinging to an inefficient way, but more importantly, I kept myself from learning a much better way of doing something. I'm grateful I had this experience relatively early, so I could learn firsthand the beauty of being a beginner.

Don't be intimidated by difficult or complex goals, instead accomplish them through "baby steps."

The way to accomplish anything difficult is to start from the beginning, break down the task into small, manageable steps, and stick with it until you reach the goal. When you are learning something and you get stuck, go back to the point where you last really understood it, review the material and move forward again once you understand it. Re-take a class if necessary. Similarly, when you are training for a marathon for the first time, you start out running just a few miles a day and build up distance over time. By sticking with something and gaining experience and expertise over time, goals that seem insurmountable become attainable. The trick is to break down the work into manageable chunks and then just keep at it. This is how novels are written, new languages learned, businesses started, marathons run, black belts achieved, PhDs awarded, etc.

Recognize that you don't have to follow your biological imperatives.

It's important to recognize and understand our biological impulses and then choose to follow them…or not! Our body has biological imperatives that were necessary for survival in earlier times but that are no longer useful. In fact, following these impulses can actually make us pretty unhappy. For instance, we are wired to gorge on food even when we are no longer hungry because when food was scarce it was beneficial to store as much fat as possible because it wasn't known when we would eat again. These days in the West, where food is so readily available, this instinct no longer serves us and it certainly doesn't lead to our happiness. Today we may want to eat an entire bag of chips but we won't feel happy if we follow that impulse. Not only will we feel queasy from all the chips, we'll also feel physically and psychically uncomfortable when we gain weight from overeating.

Our bodies are also very strongly programmed to ensure the survival of the species. To this end, men are biologically wired to want to have sex with a lot of women, while women are wired to compete with each other to win the "head man." From a purely biological standpoint, the male of our species can ensure the survival of his lineage by impregnating as many women as possible. This maximizes the number of progeny he has and the statistical chance that some will survive and go on to produce children of their own. For the female, the way to maximize the survival of her children is to have a person who can provide food and protection for her children while she is partially incapacitated by pregnancy or taking care of small children. The more capable the man is at providing and protecting, the more likely her children are to survive, thus the incentive for women to get the most capable or "head man."

Certainly, there is much more behind our decision making and actions than our biology. There is our mind and its will, as well as our soul and its longings. However, it is useful to recognize that there are hundreds of thousands of years of conditioning hardwired into our species to act out these imperatives. The biological impulses to overeat, for men to have sex unlimitedly and for women to compete with each other, can still arise in our default conditioned behavior. It's important to know our bodies have these impulses so we understand where the drives are coming from and then we can choose to follow them or not. For many, simply the recognition of these drives begins the liberation from them.

Bring your full attention to what you do.

With the advent of email, cellphones, text messaging, the Internet, etc. there are numerous ways for our focus to be interrupted. But when our attention is diffused, we don't approach our interactions with people or our work with the same level of energy and intent that we do when we are focused. When we approach people in a scattered way, we don't hear, understand and ultimately relate to them as well. When we approach work without our full attention, our work is not as clear and crisp, it takes longer to do and is not as satisfying to do as when we are focused. Even watching a movie while multi-tasking diminishes the experience. A movie takes you on an emotional journey, but when you switch your attention to texts, emails and phone conversations, your attention is leached out and the movie isn't as funny, poignant or thrilling. In other words, when you don't bring your attention to what you do, you miss all the good stuff. When you bring your full attention to work, play and relationships, they're more intense, enjoyable and satisfying.

Have integrity.

> "
> You are only afraid if you are not in harmony with yourself."
> Hermann Hesse

Lying, cheating or stealing for personal gain may give you a short-term feeling of happiness, but over the long run these actions will make you very unhappy. While these actions may not always hurt others, they will always hurt you. When you act without integrity, you end up spending an enormous amount of energy denying the actions were wrong—either by constantly pushing them out of your mind or by thinking things like, "They can afford it," "She won't really notice," or "They deserve it." The problem is when an action doesn't have integrity, it will continually rise to the surface and niggle at you and prevent you from having a happy, peaceful mind.

If it makes you sad, turn it off...

If watching a romantic comedy makes you pine for the perfect relationship and you didn't feel this painful longing before watching, then don't watch that kind of movie. If a song makes you miss an old lover or makes you sad in some way, then don't listen to it. It's so simple. There's no rule written anywhere that you have to feel sad or suffer over the past. If a song, movie, book, TV show, etc. makes you feel unhappy, turn it off. Although it's true that some people love their pain and love to indulge in sadness, you don't have to.

Limit TV time.

Watching TV is a passive activity that keeps us from living our own lives, from going out and experiencing ourselves the stories that show up on TV. This in itself is reason enough to turn it off, however a more compelling reason to turn off the TV is that it is incredibly draining and dulling. Do an experiment to fact check this for yourself. When you are feeling really upbeat and full of things you want to do, sit down and watch TV. After you have been watching for an hour, check your state of mind and see if you still feel that energy of potential. For most people, after they've been watching TV they feel really dull. Not bad, just uninspired and flat. This is not a happy feeling.

There are a lot of great TV shows these days, so this tip is not a knock against them, rather it's simply helpful to know that watching TV is draining so you can properly manage your TV consumption by 1) limiting the amount you watch and 2) properly timing when you do watch. You shouldn't watch TV before you need to do activities that require inspired energy like school work, art work, writing, etc. Get the work of the day done first, then watch TV once no more "brain power" is required for the day.

> "I don't watch TV."
> Jim Lehrer
> Anchor of PBS NewsHour from 1975-2011 and author of 20 novels, 3 plays and 2 memoirs, when asked how he accomplished so much.

Watch out for other media that make you feel weird or bad. For example, most fashion magazines will make you feel icky in short order.

Reduce your time on the Internet.

The Internet is a tremendous depressant. After spending fifteen or twenty minutes reading the web, you feel less energized, less hopeful and worst of all, less motivated, regardless of the content you're reading! Fact check this for yourself. When you are feeling good one morning, write down your state of mind and what you feel like doing for the day, then surf the Internet for twenty minutes. Next, look at your state of mind. How do you feel—do you feel differently than you did twenty minutes ago? Most people find that surfing the Internet takes their edge away. The remedy is to be quick and efficient when doing online banking or shopping transactions and to reduce the amount of time spent reading and watching mindless "entertainment." You can even download information from the Internet and read it offline. I promise you will feel better if you follow this tip!

Don't own other people's thoughts and feelings.

A large portion of the thoughts and feelings you have are not yours, rather you pick them up from others. This may seem entirely shocking and untrue, but you can do an experiment to fact check this for yourself. Go for a hike alone on an *uncrowded* trail and take note of the number of thoughts you have. After you have been hiking for an hour or so, you'll notice your mind is very still and that you don't have many thoughts. Next go to a mall or someplace crowded and walk around for a while and observe how many thoughts are running through your mind. In a crowded place you'll notice your mind becomes very loud and full of thoughts.

It's helpful to be aware of this phenomenon because if you're around an angry person, you'll notice that you'll begin to have angry thoughts. If you're around someone who is worried about money, you'll be worried about money. If you spend a lot of time with someone who is depressed, you'll feel tired or hopeless when you're around them. When you realize that a lot of the things that you think and feel aren't coming from you, you can be an "educated consumer" and not spend as much time with people or in places where you pick up crappy thoughts and feelings. You can also learn to not act on the emotions that you pick up externally that aren't yours.

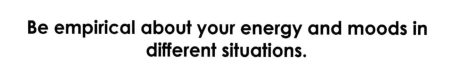

Be empirical about your energy and moods in different situations.

Notice which people, situations or activities energize or drain you. Notice how you feel before interactions and how you feel afterwards. Take note of the patterns so you can become consciously aware of the situations and activities that give you energy or that drain you. By being truly aware of what is draining and what is empowering, we can make better decisions about where we spend our time.

Keep a to-do list.

This is such a simple technique that it's almost laughable, but writing down the things you need to do helps keep your mind quiet. It frees your mind from having to remember to do something. Every morning when you are clear from your morning meditation, you can look at your to-do list, prioritize it and pick the top things you want to do. This keeps you focused on what is really important to you and prevents you from getting side-tracked by things that are non-essential. This technique is even more valuable now that we have so many time-sinks around to distract us.

> "
> Our life is frittered away by detail....
> Simplify, simplify."
> *Walden*
> Henry D. Thoreau

Simplify your life.

Simplify your life so you have time to do the things you really love and that make you happy. Remove unnecessary and dull activities and relationships from your life. Also, look at the things you do out of obligation that you dislike and realistically assess whether you need to do them or not.

Take a hike.
Get out of town.

Get out in nature, away from people, at least once a month, as this will slow down the activity of the mind and clear you out. You'll feel better and be able to see things about your life more clearly.

Similarly, get out of town for a few nights every few months or so. Everything will be brighter and clearer when you return home. Many times, the solution to a problem will become clear and sometimes a problem will cease to even exist because the issue that previously felt like a big deal will no longer feel like a problem.

Stop caring what other people think of you.

People perceiving you as rich, beautiful, lucky, tough or smart will not make you happy, yet you wouldn't know this if you observed how much time and energy people spend trying to get other people to think they are those things. If people think you have got it made, it won't make you happy. Just look at celebrities—many people admire them and think they have it made, but clearly it doesn't make them happy. In fact, given the number of divorces and trips to rehab, you could posit they are one of the least happy segments of the population. So stop being concerned with what other people think of you, it's a waste of your energy and keeps you from having a quiet mind.

Don't judge others.

Judging and being critical of others is a waste of your energy. It doesn't change the target of your judgement, and instead it fills your mind with critical sentiments that do not feel good or happy.

When people are rude or mean to you, it's usually not personal, but instead a reflection of their own mind state.

When the cashier at the grocery store is rude to you or someone at work tries to belittle your work, most times their behavior has nothing to do with you, but instead is a reflection of their own state of mind. That cashier is rude to everyone and that coworker tries to make everyone feel small. It helps to know this so we don't take it personally and let it affect our mood.

> "I don't care what you think about me. I don't think about you at all."
> Coco Chanel

The way you don't let troublesome people get to you, is to be indifferent to them.

This doesn't mean you become numb or indifferent to everyone, simply be indifferent and have no emotional openings to those who cause you pain, for example an ex-boyfriend or ex-girlfriend or a relative who is a jerk.

Drop the desire/aversion approach to life.

Most people spend an enormous amount of energy trying to attract the things they desire and repel the things they are averse to. The things most people want to attract are relationship, money, success and recognition. The things most people try to keep away are the things they are afraid of or that make them uncomfortable, such as being alone, unloved, in pain, or appearing dumb or unsuccessful. In this desire/aversion approach, the basis of our thoughts and actions revolve around trying to get what we desire and avoid what we are averse to.

The problem with this approach is twofold. First, it's not a very reliable approach because if your happiness is based on getting what you want and avoiding what you don't want, you're bound to be unhappy a lot of the time! We can look at our own lives and the people around us and see that the world just doesn't go our way a lot of the time. And even when we do get what we want, the happiness that it creates can be very transient. The new car (or house, or job, or boyfriend/girlfriend/husband/wife) that you wanted may turn out to not be what you expected, or after you have had it for a while it's not as exciting; you get used to it and it no longer thrills you, or you wreck it and that makes you unhappy. In all these cases, the happiness brought on by these things should absolutely be enjoyed, but they should be recognized as undependable sources of lasting happiness.

Second, this desire/aversion approach to happiness consumes an enormous amount of mental energy. All of the strategizing, scheming and avoiding required to bring what you desire and repel what you don't, creates a busy mind which blocks you from seeing and feeling your innate light. So paradoxically, all the mental activity devoted to getting what you want so you'll be happy, actually makes you feel less happy.

Dropping the desire/aversion approach to life doesn't mean you don't try to achieve things, it just means you don't look to those achievements for intrinsic, lasting happiness. They are fun, many times worth doing or having, just don't expect them to be your ultimate source of happiness. And happily, when you stop clinging so tightly to the things you desire, you actually enjoy them more because you're not so afraid of losing them.

The alternative to this system is to get your happiness from the light of eternity. When you go into the light you can't help but get a smile on your face. After meditating you can do the most mundane things and be radiantly happy because you feel that light in your being. From this place, when good things happen to you, you can enjoy them and when bad things happen, your boat won't be so rocked by the world not going your way. After some years of meditation, your happiness will barely be affected by what's going on in the world. This might sound so strange as to not even be appealing, but I can tell you it's the best place to be. You're not unrealistic about what is going on in the world, nor are you spaced out or ungrounded, you are simply getting your happiness from light instead of from things working out in the world.

Small Tips and Ideas

1. Keep on hand at all times great audio books, podcasts, music, books or magazines. It's helpful to have something entertaining to do when you are waiting in line at the DMV or at the doctor's office or when you're caught in traffic or on the subway. There are so many draining situations that become the opposite when you have something interesting to occupy your mind.

2. Likewise, have high-vibe hobbies and projects to focus on in your spare time. The mind takes on the vibration of whatever you focus on, so you'll feel happier when the places you put your mind are "high-vibe" and happy. Avoid putting your mind in "low-vibe" places like certain video games, pornography or certain parts of the Internet. This tip is not coming from a moralistic viewpoint at all, rather it's intended to help you become an educated consumer by pointing out that these types of entertainment make most people feel crappy, annoyed or dull after engaging in them.

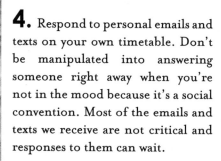

3. Control when you read potentially toxic emails by segregating your email accounts. Give people who can adversely affect your mood a different email address than your primary one, and only check the alternate address when you feel up to it.

4. Respond to personal emails and texts on your own timetable. Don't be manipulated into answering someone right away when you're not in the mood because it's a social convention. Most of the emails and texts we receive are not critical and responses to them can wait.

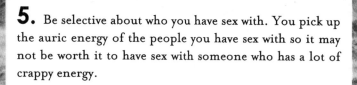

5. Be selective about who you have sex with. You pick up the auric energy of the people you have sex with so it may not be worth it to have sex with someone who has a lot of crappy energy.

6. Be kind to yourself. Eat well, get enough sleep and invest in self-care, such as massages and baths. Be compassionate with yourself!

7. Resist the urge to explain yourself. It's draining and most times it's more information than people are interested in anyway.

8. Eat a protein-based breakfast. Protein keeps you grounded and makes it easier to handle the stressful energies of the day.

9. If someone is tailgating you, change lanes or pull over to let them pass. Tailgaters press on you energetically and it's tiring. Similarly, don't tailgate and press your energy on the person in front of you. Take a deep breath, relax and ease off the accelerator for a moment.

10. Hassle the details. A tremendous amount of energy and trouble is saved when you pay your bills on time, get directions before you leave for a new location, review important documents/statements in a timely manner, etc.

11. Don't overuse your alarm's Snooze button. The Snooze button largely backfires because the 8 or 9 additional minutes of sleep you get usually make you feel more groggy rather than less.

12. Park your shoes at the door and switch into comfy house slippers. Leave the energy of the outside world at your door.

13. Have your own room, either a bedroom, studio or office space, that is just yours and where you only feel your energy.

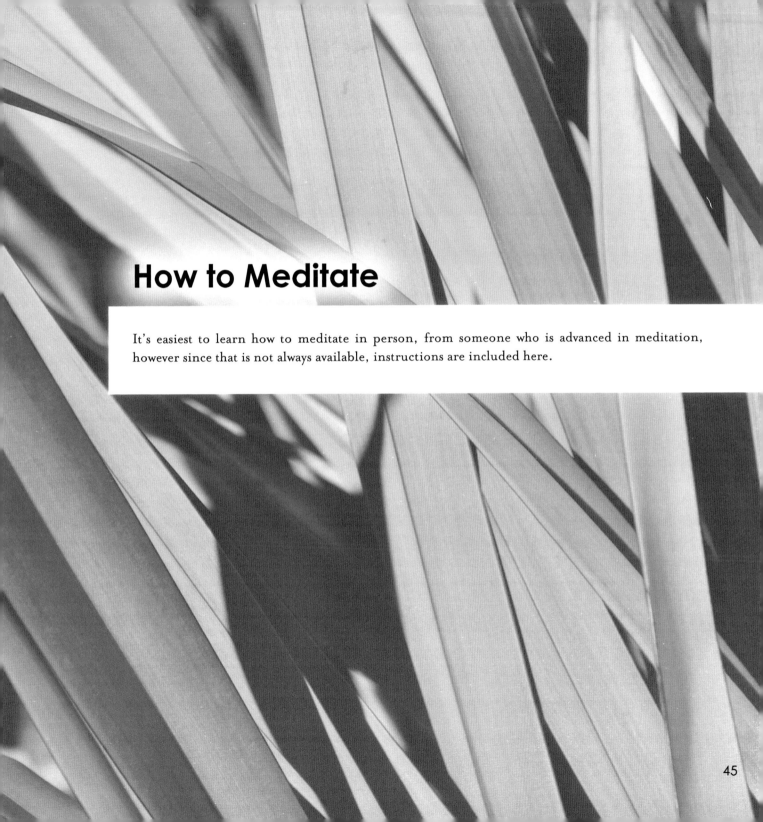

How to Meditate

It's easiest to learn how to meditate in person, from someone who is advanced in meditation, however since that is not always available, instructions are included here.

Things to Know Before You Get Started

Best Times to Meditate

In the morning, meditate shortly after you wake up. It's easier to meditate when you feel awake and alert, so take a shower (or at least wash your hands and face) and have a cup of coffee, tea or juice if you need that. A few bites of food are fine, but avoid eating a meal because a full stomach makes meditating more difficult. You will also have an easier time quieting your mind if you meditate before you engage your mind in the things that start it spinning, such as email, TV, Internet, phone calls or other conversations.

In the evening, you can meditate at sunset, when you get home, or before you go to bed. The sunset meditation is especially nice, when you can make it. Again, shower or wash your hands and face before you sit down.

Meditation Attire

Wear clean, comfortable clothes that won't physically distract you while you are meditating. Also, it's nice to have clothes that you use just for meditation, so they don't have any other associations, such as work, with them.

Meditation Area

Meditate in an area that is clean and bright and is yours alone. The space should only be used for meditation. So for instance, if you meditate in a corner of your bedroom, don't do anything else in that corner. You can have just your cushion or chair there, or you can also have additional items that inspire you like a picture or flowers.

Posture

You can meditate either in a chair or on the floor in half-lotus (see illustration on page 49) or cross-legged. Choose whichever position is most comfortable for you. One is not better than the other, what matters is that you keep your back very straight, with a curve in the small of your back. Your shoulders should be down and relaxed. Your neck should be in line with your spine with your head forward and not tilting up or down. If you sit in a chair, this posture is more easily achieved if you sit towards the front of the chair rather than rest your back against the chair back. If you sit on the floor, it's helpful to sit on a cushion, with your hips higher than your knees. You can find numerous meditation cushions for sale online. The ones filled with buckwheat hulls are especially nice because they conform to your shape and allow better circulation, which helps keep your legs from falling asleep.

You should not meditate lying down, except in cases of illness or accident, because it's almost impossible to not get too relaxed and fall asleep.

Your Hands

Your hands can rest in your lap, on your knees or be in one of the traditional meditation *mudras*. Just do whatever feels natural and comfortable.

Length

Start out meditating for fifteen minutes in the morning and, if you can, fifteen minutes at night. After a few months or so you can increase your time to thirty minutes and then gradually work up to an hour long session, both morning and evening. You will easily know when it is time to lengthen your meditation session because it's when you find you want to sit longer.

Privacy

Be sure to turn your phone ringer off so you won't be disturbed during your meditation. Also, let the members of your household know to not bother you when you are meditating.

Meditation Techniques

All meditation techniques are about stilling the mind—about replacing the myriad of thoughts in your mind with one thought, and then eventually, no thoughts. Below are several techniques that help still the mind. Many people find the easiest technique to start with is chakra meditation with music, because the right music can make meditation easier. You may want to try them all out first to see which you like best.

There's not a set time when you should switch to using another technique. You may rotate through the techniques on a daily or weekly basis, or you may do only the chakra meditation for the first two years. There is no one right approach—what matters is meditating on a regular basis and being able to slow down the mind. Whatever mix of techniques helps you achieve that is the best approach!

Chakra Meditation

In this technique you focus on your chakras as the means to still your mind, so first a brief description of what chakras are, where they are located and the benefit of focusing on them.

The chakras—the body of light that surrounds your physical body is called the subtle body. It is composed of a network of filaments, or fibers of light, that join at places called chakras. There are seven primary chakras and though they are in your subtle body, they correspond to physical locations in the body, starting at the base of your spine and continuing up to the top of your head.

The first chakra is located at the base of the spine and is called the root chakra. The second chakra is located where your sex organs are. The third chakra is your navel center. It is about an inch below your belly button and is the chakra that is focused on first in this technique.

The navel chakra is the chakra of power. When you focus on a chakra you release the energy that is associated with the chakra, so when you focus on the navel center you increase the amount of willpower you have, which makes it easier to make things happen in your life.

The fourth chakra is the heart chakra. It's located in the center of your chest and is the chakra of balance and love. In this technique you will focus on this chakra second. When you focus here you bring more happiness, love and balance into your life.

The next chakra is the throat chakra which is at the base of the throat. It's the center of creativity. You will not specifically focus on this chakra, however when you focus on the heart chakra, you also activate the throat chakra.

The sixth chakra is the third eye. It's located just between your eyebrows and slightly above. It is the center of knowledge and wisdom and is the third chakra focused on in this technique.

The seventh chakra is at the top of the head and is called the crown center. It takes some years of meditation to activate the crown chakra, so it's not focused on starting out.

The technique—in this technique you are going to focus on three chakras, however not simultaneously. For the first third of the meditation, you are going to focus on the navel center. The second third, you will focus on the heart chakra, and finally for the last third of the meditation you will focus on the third eye.

So first, when you start meditating, focus on your navel center. Close your eyes and feel the spot with your mind. Focus on the chakra to the exclusion of everything else. When you're starting out you can hold your fingers on the chakra to help bring your attention to the spot.

After a third of your meditation session time, move your attention to your heart chakra. Focus here to the exclusion of everything else. Again, when you are starting out, you can hold your fingertips on the chakra if it helps you.

For the last third of your meditation session, move your focus to the third eye and feel the area with your mind. As your mind starts to wander, gently bring your focus back to the area.

When you are focusing on the chakras, you may see colors, feel sensations of lightness or simply just feel happy. While it's fun to experience these sensations, it's important to refocus on the chakra because when you begin to think about what you're experiencing you stop meditating!

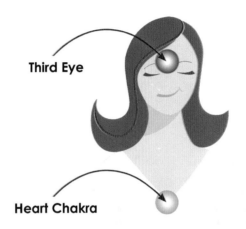

Third Eye

Heart Chakra

Navel Center

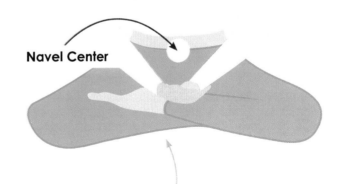

This posture is called **half-lotus**. In it, one foot rests on top of your calf, while the other foot is underneath your thigh.

Chakra Meditation with Music

The chakra technique described above can be practiced with music, which is highly recommended. Music helps buffer you from the distractions and noise of the outside world. When you meditate to music, focus on the chakra to the exclusion of everything else, then when you find your attention wandering, shift your focus to the music and focus on it while still keeping a light focus on the chakra. You can follow an instrument or just listen deeply to the music. When your attention starts to wander again, shift your focus back to the chakra. Alternate between the music and the chakra until your meditation is complete. Starting out, hold your focus on the chakra for about 40 seconds before you switch your focus to the music, then hold your focus on the music for about 40 seconds before you switch back to the chakra. Over time work up to several minutes of focus on the chakra before switching focus to the music, and vice versa.

If noise is a problem in your environment, it's extremely helpful to use headphones while meditating.

Yantra Meditation

A yantra is a geometric design that you focus on to quiet your mind. Focus on the dot at the center of the yantra, to the exclusion of everything else, for the entire meditation session. A really nice yantra for meditation is the Sri yantra, pictured here. You can find one online.

Mantra Meditation

Mantra meditation is the repetition of a mantra through the entirety of your meditation session. A great mantra for anyone to use in meditation is *Om mani padme hum*. It means the jewel in the lotus, and is a poetic way of saying that enlightenment is inside of everything and everyone (including you!). The mantra can be repeated aloud or chanted inwardly. Be sure to focus your full attention on the mantra and not just repeat it mechanically.

Chakra Meditation with Mantra

While repeating the mantra, inwardly or aloud, hold a light focus on your naval center for the first third of the meditation, the heart chakra for the middle third, and the third eye for the last part of your meditation session.

During your Meditation Session

When you catch yourself thinking, be it about what you're going to eat for breakfast, what you need to do today or even about how much you're thinking, simply bring your focus back to the chakra, yantra or mantra. Don't get mad at yourself because that's just another thought! Just ignore the thoughts and be patient with yourself. Our minds are used to thinking and traveling all over the map, so it takes some time and patience to learn how to meditate well.

At the End of Your Session

Bow and sit quietly for a few minutes to allow the silence to sink in fully.

Additional Meditation Tips

Don't judge your meditation.

It's important to not judge your meditation. The only bad meditation is the one you don't do! The truth is even when you have meditations that don't feel as "good" or "powerful" as others, the light is still transforming you. It's still working, even if it doesn't feel like a good meditation to you. That being said you need to meditate correctly.

You need to **meditate correctly** for it to really work.

Meditate correctly.

If you just space out and let your mind wander, you won't experience the benefits of meditation. In order to meditate correctly, it's important to not think about other people or talk to other people in your mind. Don't work on your to-do list or ruminate on projects at work or school. Instead, when you notice you are thinking, simply bring your focus back to the chakra (or to the music, mantra or yantra). Don't fight the thought or get frustrated that you are thinking, again, be patient with yourself and just return your mind to the area of focus.

Also keep in mind that a shorter, completely focused meditation is more effective than a longer, spaced-out one.

Mix it up.

Don't get stuck doing your meditation practice the same way all the time. What works best for you will change over time.

Albums for Meditation

When looking for good meditation music, keep in mind that while New Age music is nice to meditate to, a lot of it can make you really sleepy when you meditate. You need to be picky—if something makes you sleepy, you need to look for other albums that don't make you fall asleep while meditating. Also be aware that sometimes an album will work well for a while and then quit working. At that point you need to find new music and not hold on to the hope that it will start working for you again.

Sleeping, while necessary for a healthy mind and body, is not considered meditation.

If You Hit a Plateau...

If you reach a point where you are not going higher or deeper in your meditation, it's helpful to find a teacher who is more advanced than you are. A good teacher can see what is keeping you from going higher and can provide correction and direction.

There are some good teachers out there and some bad, unknowledgeable or unethical ones. In order to find the right one for you, you have to trust your non-physical body. If something feels wrong in your "gut," you should leave. At the same time, you need to be aware that a good teacher, as part of the correction and direction to assist you in going higher, may tell you things you won't necessarily want to hear and that make you feel uncomfortable. So if you feel the urge to leave a teacher, you need to check that it's because something feels intuitively wrong with the teacher, and not because you want to run away from unpleasant truths.

Resources

For more resources and tips visit how2behappyblog.com.

About the Author

Sara Weston has been meditating for over twenty years and is happy all the time, even when things aren't going her way.